CAREER CONVERSATIONS

Volume 1 - Empower to be Empowered

RK BODDU

ISBN 979-8-89322-984-4

This book is dedicated to parents, students, and career mentors alike, who embark on the transformative journey of career exploration and guidance. Within these pages, you will find a wealth of insights, anecdotes, and reflections aimed at empowering individuals of all ages to navigate the intricacies of career development with clarity, confidence, and purpose.

For parents, this book serves as a guiding light, offering valuable perspectives on nurturing their children's aspirations, fostering open dialogue, and embracing the uniqueness of their journey. Through shared experiences and practical advice, parents gain the tools and insights needed to support their children's career aspirations while fostering a nurturing and empowering environment.

To students, "Career Conversations" offers a roadmap for self-discovery, exploration, and growth. From crystallizing aspirations to confronting challenges, each section of this book provides valuable insights and practical guidance to help students navigate the complexities of career planning with resilience and determination.

For career mentors, this book serves as a source of inspiration and reflection, offering new perspectives on guiding and empowering the next generation of professionals. Through shared experiences and thought-provoking insights, mentors gain valuable tools and strategies to support their mentees on their journey toward professional fulfillment.

As you embark on this journey through "Career Conversations," may you find inspiration, guidance, and encouragement to embrace your unique path toward professional fulfillment. Together, let us empower each other to be empowered, and embark on a transformative journey toward realizing our career aspirations.

Contents

SECTION 3: ECCENTRIC EXPECTATIONS

SECTION 4: PARENTING PATTERNS

SECTION 5: PRUDENT PLANNING

SECTION 6: PERSONAL ANECDOTES

SECTION 7: OUT OF BOUNDS

Preface

After nearly twenty years immersed in the corporate world of information technology within multinational corporations, I found myself at a crossroads, seeking to embark on a mid-career revival. Transitioning into the role of a career mentor, I have spent the past six years navigating this new path.

During my journey as a mentor, I have had the privilege of engaging in countless conversations with students, parents, and fellow mentors from various corners of the country. Through these interactions, I have witnessed the power of guidance and support in helping young individuals and their families make informed decisions about their futures.

Driven by a sense of responsibility and a desire to share the insights gleaned from these conversations, I felt compelled to compile them into this book. While these conversations have previously been shared through my YouTube and podcast channels, I believe that their value can be further amplified through the written word.

Through the pages of this book, I hope to distill the essence of these conversations and experiences, offering readers a comprehensive guide to navigating the complexities of career development. Together, let us embark on a journey of empowerment, enlightenment, and growth.

With gratitude and anticipation,
RK Boddu

Introduction

Welcome to "Career Conversations: Volume 1 - Empower to Be Empowered"!

This book is a testament to the power of dialogue, mentorship, and self-discovery in the journey toward professional fulfillment. Within these pages, you will find a tapestry of stories, insights, and reflections that illuminate the diverse pathways individuals navigate as they seek to realize their career aspirations.

In a world characterized by rapid change and evolving opportunities, the pursuit of a meaningful and fulfilling career has never been more complex. From students forging their paths to parents navigating aspirations and mentors guiding the next generation, "Career Conversations" delves into the heart of these transformative dialogues, offering perspectives that inspire, inform, and empower.

The title, "Empower to Be Empowered," encapsulates the essence of the book's mission—to ignite a ripple effect of empowerment that cascades through generations. Each conversation shared within these pages serves as a catalyst for growth, resilience, and self-realization, embodying the transformative power of mentorship and collaboration.

Through the diverse narratives and perspectives shared within these pages, "Career Conversations" seeks to empower individuals to chart their unique paths, embrace their passions, and navigate the complexities of the professional world with confidence and purpose.

As you engage with the narratives and perspectives shared within these pages, you may find inspiration, guidance, and encouragement to embark on your own path toward professional fulfillment.

This book is a compilation of 29 authentic conversations, divided into 7 sections, each offering a unique perspective on the complexities of career decision-making. From the clarity of early aspirations to the limitations encountered along the way, these conversations provide invaluable insights into the challenges and triumphs of shaping one's professional path.

Structured into 7 thematic sections, the book traverses the landscape of career development, offering insights and reflections that resonate with individuals at every stage of their professional journey.

Section 1. Crystal Clear:

In this section, we delve into the importance of clarity in career aspirations. Through insightful conversations and personal anecdotes, readers explore the process of discovering and articulating their professional goals with conviction and clarity.

Section 2. Clutter to Clarity:

Navigating through the clutter of societal expectations, familial influences, and personal aspirations is a journey fraught with challenges. In this section, readers are invited to untangle the complexities of their career paths and emerge with a newfound sense of clarity and purpose.

Section 3. Eccentric Expectations:

Breaking free from conventional career norms, embracing eccentric aspirations, and challenging societal expectations are themes explored in this section. Through engaging narratives, readers are encouraged to embrace their uniqueness and chart unconventional paths to success.

Section 4. Parenting Patterns:

The influence of parental expectations, cultural norms, and familial dynamics on career choices is examined in this section. From navigating parental pressures to forging independent paths, readers gain insights into the complexities of parent-child relationships in the context of career development.

Section 5. Prudent Planning:

Planning for the future, navigating uncertainty, and embracing opportunities are central themes of this section. Through practical advice and strategic insights, readers learn the importance of prudent planning and foresight in achieving their professional aspirations.

Section 6. Personal Anecdotes:

In this section, personal stories and anecdotes offer glimpses into the diverse experiences and perspectives that shape individual career journeys. Through shared narratives, readers find solace, inspiration, and wisdom in the collective wisdom of their peers.

Section 7. Out of Bounds:

Confronting limitations, overcoming obstacles, and embracing resilience are explored in this section. Through tales of perseverance and triumph, readers are reminded of the inherent power within themselves to transcend boundaries and achieve their dreams.

Section 1

Crystal Clear

01

Early Start

During my counseling and mentoring sessions, I encountered an intriguing situation involving a seventh-grade student from a prominent international school in Chennai. What struck me was the school's forward-thinking approach—they encouraged career conversations 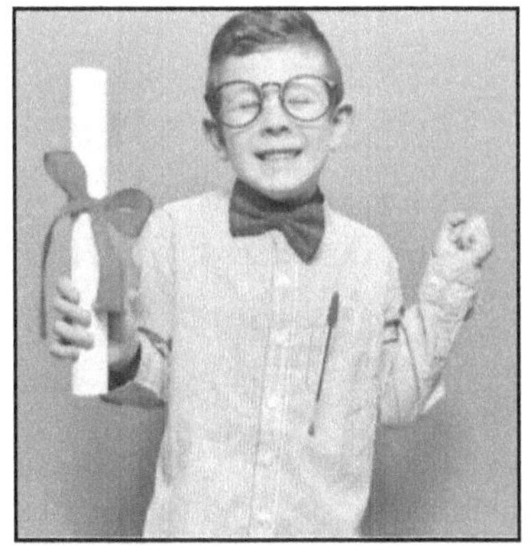 as early as sixth grade. This proactive stance aligns with practices in some other countries as well.

Now, let me share the story of this seventh grader. With unwavering clarity, he approached me and declared, "Sir, my name is so-and-so, and I aspire to pursue a career in space science. Specifically, I want to delve into astrophysics and astronomy. Becoming a space researcher is my ultimate goal."

It's heartening to witness young minds aiming for the stars, quite literally.

In a remarkable turn of events, this seventh-grade student approached me for college planning advice. His eagerness to prepare early caught my attention. Most schools in India don't initiate career conversations until later grades, but this forward-thinking institution encouraged students to explore their paths from an early age.

The young boy was crystal clear about his aspirations: he wanted to pursue space science, specifically astrophysics and astronomy. His unwavering commitment impressed me. Soon, his father joined our conversation, reinforcing their shared enthusiasm for this unique career choice.

As a career counselor, my job becomes significantly easier when both parents and children are aligned in their aspirations.

As we discussed college planning, I learned that the boy had even visited a NASA space station during a trip to the United States. His passion for space research had ignited early, and as counselors, we were there to guide him toward the stars.

During our discussion, I emphasized the importance of building a strong profile. Beyond academic excellence, he needed to engage in extracurricular and co-curricular activities. We explored various avenues, from participating in science fairs to attending seminars and securing internships related to space science.

This experience reaffirmed the value of early exploration. While some students remain uncertain even in 11th or 12th grade, this young visionary exemplified the power of clarity from an early age. As educators, we must encourage curiosity and guide young minds toward fulfilling their dreams.

> *"Your career is like a garden. It needs to be cultivated and nurtured early on to blossom into something beautiful."*

Unconventional Choice

During one of my counseling sessions with a group of eighth and ninth-grade students, an unexpected question arose. A girl from Tamil Nadu, studying in the ninth grade, stood up and asked, "Sir, can you discuss reptile breeding as a potential career?" Her curiosity caught me off guard, and I realized that sometimes the most unconventional questions come from the most unexpected places.

I found myself taken aback by an unexpected inquiry during this career conversation. Two aspects surprised me: first, her choice of topic—reptile breeding—was unconventional, especially for a girl. Second, while I had a general understanding of reptile breeding, I lacked specific details about courses, colleges, career prospects, and earning potential.

To gain some time, I asked if her parents were aware of her career interests, and she confirmed that they were. I decided to revisit the topic during our next session, where I could provide more informed guidance. Sometimes, even as a counselor, I encounter questions that stretch beyond the ordinary, prompting me to explore new avenues of knowledge.

The following day, the same group of students and their parents reconvened for our career discussion. To my surprise, one of the parents asked, "Can you talk about reptile breeding as a career?" I quickly recalled the girl who had posed the same question the previous day. It turned out that she was the parent's daughter, and both were enthusiastic about her pursuing this unconventional path.

Having done my homework the night before, I delved into the topic. I explained the courses, pathways, and prospects related to reptile breeding. Interestingly, while this field wasn't widely popular in India, it enjoyed significant recognition outside the country. I also highlighted the existence of a black market for reptile breeding, where substantial sums were involved. Legally, it was permissible in many countries, but aspiring professionals might need to explore opportunities beyond India.

In the end, they left with a clearer understanding of this unique career choice. Sometimes, unexpected questions lead us to fascinating discoveries.

As a counselor, I've encountered students who surprise me with their unconventional career choices. As in this instance of a young girl interested in reptile breeding as a career. Her unexpected query reminded me that sometimes the most remarkable paths lie beyond our imagination.

As parents and mentors, we should encourage our children to explore diverse possibilities. After all, the sky is the limit, and unconventional careers can lead to extraordinary experiences. Eventually, they'll find their own path, guided by both curiosity and practical considerations.

"Remember, sometimes the path less traveled leads to remarkable discoveries."

03

Expectations vs Possibilities

I have an intriguing insight to share this time - it's about expectations versus possibilities. Picture this: I encountered a 12th-grade student deeply immersed in PCM (Physics, Chemistry, Mathematics) studies, gearing up for JEE, BITSAT, and other entrance exams.

Both the child and the parent were fixated on the idea of the child pursuing electronics and communication in engineering. They based this decision on the child's active participation in electronics projects during school science fairs and extracurricular activities.

But here's the twist: they sought professional guidance to validate their plan and explore other avenues. We conducted thorough psychometric assessments indicating the child's affinity for hands-on, equipment-oriented tasks, aligning well with electronics. However, we wanted to delve deeper.

I introduced the student to a visualization exercise, a process where dreams meet reality. As the student visualized his future, he crafted a compelling vision statement: "I aim to invent an interplanetary communication device, earning international recognition for my innovation."

This vision statement stunned the parent, whose expectations were modest - secure admission, get a job, settle down. Witnessing the child's grand vision, the parent was moved to tears, overwhelmed by the untapped potential. It was a poignant moment, a realization that their child's aspirations transcended conventional expectations.

This experience underscores a crucial point: while parents may set expectations, a child's possibilities are boundless. As mentors, our role is to nurture and empower, guiding them to explore their potential. Let's not confine them to our limited expectations; instead, let's inspire them to reach for the stars.

In essence, the journey from expectations to possibilities is transformative. It's about embracing the unknown, fostering a mindset where the sky's not the limit - it's just the beginning.

Whether you're a counselor, parent, or student, may this story resonate and inspire you to embrace the infinite possibilities that lie ahead.

"Don't limit yourself. Many people limit themselves to what they think they can do. You can go as far as your mind lets you. What you believe, remember, you can achieve."

Section 2

Clutter to Clarity

04

Anxious Planning

During a visit to a prominent school in Hyderabad known for its exclusive focus on international curriculum, I conducted a career workshop for parents and children of 8th to 10th grades. The session, which lasted for an hour, delved into intense and intriguing discussions, particularly during the question-and-answer segment.

In the midst of the workshop, a parent, who hadn't been formally invited, entered the auditorium seeking guidance.

Despite their child being in sixth grade, well before the typical focus of career discussions, they expressed a keen interest in exploring curriculum options like CBSE, ICSE, IB, or Cambridge. This unexpected inquiry prompted me to inquire about the school's existing curriculum, considering their child was already enrolled in the sixth grade.

He mentioned that it was for his younger child, and I assumed the child was perhaps in the fifth grade or facing the dilemma of changing boards or selecting a different curriculum, prompting me to inquire about the child's age and grade level. To my surprise, he revealed that his younger child hadn't even started formal schooling yet and was currently attending a preschool. The parent expressed a desire to make an informed choice about which curriculum would be best suited for his child, despite the child not yet being enrolled in a formal school.

This revelation was surprising and shocking, as it seemed unusual for a parent of a preschooler to be evaluating different curriculum options. However, I acknowledged the parent's cautious approach and proceeded to discuss the merits and drawbacks of various curricula such as CBSE, CIB, Cambridge, and others. I emphasized that each curriculum serves a specific purpose and is designed to meet particular requirements. It's akin to comparing apples and oranges - they serve different purposes, and one cannot expect the same outcome from both.

During our 10 to 15-minute conversation, I provided insights into the objectives, strengths, and weaknesses of each curriculum, helping the parent understand the nuances and guiding principles behind their designs. By the end of our discussion, the parent seemed satisfied and more informed about the available options.

This experience highlighted the level of anxiety and eagerness among parents of kindergarten or preschool-aged children to make the right educational choices. While it may seem overwhelming at times, I believe it is essential for parents to approach such decisions with caution and informed consideration, ensuring the best possible outcome for their child's education.

"Anxiety is the handmaiden of contemporary ambition."

05

Analysis Paralysis

I'd like to share an intriguing experience involving a parent from my neighborhood who recently had their second child. Their elder son is around three years old, and the younger one is a 

toddler. Knowing that I am a career counselor and also a parent of older children, they approached me for advice more as a neighbor and fellow parent than as a professional counselor.

The parent was facing a dilemma about which kindergarten to choose for their child. They had conducted extensive research, personally visiting over 40 schools in Hyderabad, and analyzing various factors, including the implications of the new education policy. Their main concerns revolved around when to admit their child and which curriculum would be best suited for them.

This situation epitomized what we call "analysis paralysis." The parent was extremely data-driven and had meticulously analyzed numerous aspects, yet they found themselves unable to make a decision.

Their specific concern was whether to admit their child to kindergarten before or after the age of three and a half. Some schools accepted children before this age, while others had a minimum age requirement of three and a half years.

I advised the parent to consider their objectives carefully. If they wanted their child to enjoy their early years and focus on sensory development before starting formal education, waiting until the next academic year might be beneficial. However, practical considerations, such as parental work commitments and childcare arrangements, also needed to be taken into account.

Ultimately, I emphasized that while thorough analysis is essential, excessive deliberation can hinder decision-making. It's crucial to strike a balance between analysis and practicality. Each family's situation is unique, and what works for one may not work for another.

This experience highlighted the challenges parents face when making educational decisions for their children and the importance of seeking advice when overwhelmed by analysis.

"Over-analysis leads to paralysis."

International School

In a recent career workshop at a school, I engaged in an extensive conversation with a parent and child duo. The parent's journey from modest beginnings to financial stability was evident, paving the way for their aspirations for their child's education. They sought out an "international" school, believing it would guarantee top-tier education.

However, the chosen school, despite its "international" label, offered a CBSE curriculum, not the expected

International Baccalaureate or Cambridge international programs. The child, struggling to adapt to the CBSE syllabus, raised concerns among school authorities.

This scenario underscores a common misconception: assuming a school's name ensures educational excellence. Many parents, like this one, overlook curriculum specifics, relying solely on a school's reputation. Unfortunately, this lack of awareness led to a mismatch between expectations and reality.

The underlying message is clear: parents must align their educational goals with the school's offerings. Blindly selecting a school based on its name can lead to academic challenges for the child. Seeking guidance from experts or school counselors can offer valuable insights and prevent such pitfalls.

Furthermore, the parent's fixation on prestigious careers like medicine or engineering highlights the importance of informed decision-making. It's essential to prioritize understanding school offerings over brand recognition when choosing a child's education. Informed decisions based on awareness ensure the best educational outcomes.

The narrative unveils the significance of informed choices in shaping a child's academic journey. It underscores the need for parents to delve deeper into school offerings rather than relying solely on superficial labels. Through awareness and informed decisions, parents can set their children on paths to success in education and beyond.

> *"Don't judge a book by its cover; there's more*
> *to a person than meets the eye."*

07

U Turn

In this episode, I want to share an intriguing conversation I had with one of my mentees, a student who has completed the second year of his engineering studies. Despite coming from a humble background with limited financial resources, this student has excelled academically in computer engineering at a reputable college in his region.

Our telephonic conversation, initially intended to be brief, extended to 90 minutes due to the depth of questions and concerns raised by the student. He expressed a newfound belief that a career in medicine offered more societal respect than engineering. This perception, he explained, stemmed from the noble reputation associated with the medical profession compared to engineering.

To help him reconsider his decision, I used a metaphor of driving—a straight road being preferable to one with frequent turns or U-turns. Taking a U-turn, I emphasized, is challenging and often inconvenient, both in driving and in career choices. Despite understanding the difficulty, the student remained convinced of his desire to pursue medicine, citing his eligibility in biology, chemistry, physics, and mathematics from high school.

While advising against a complete shift, I proposed a compromise: continue with engineering studies while dedicating time to prepare for medical entrance exams. This midway approach, I believed, allowed him to maintain academic progress while exploring his medical aspirations.

Ultimately, the episode underscores the importance of making informed decisions early in one's academic journey. U-turns, whether on the road or in career paths, are challenging and should be approached with caution. Parents play a crucial role in guiding students toward thoughtful career choices that align with their interests and goals. It's essential to consider all options and weigh them carefully to avoid unnecessary disruptions and ensure a smooth academic and professional trajectory.

"It's never too late to change direction, but it's always better to do it early."

Does Education Guarantee Success

This episode delves into a familiar question: Is education necessary for success, or does having an education guarantee it? It's a query I often encounter during my career workshops and mentoring sessions, especially from young individuals questioning the relevance of formal education in their pursuit of success.

Many cite examples like Steve Jobs, Mark Zuckerberg, and Bill

Gates as evidence that success can be achieved without formal education. They view these renowned figures, all college dropouts, as proof that traditional education isn't indispensable. Such arguments present challenges for parents and mentors tasked with guiding young minds through their educational journey.

Let's examine both sides of the argument. On one hand, education undoubtedly plays a significant role in an individual's success. Academic qualifications open doors to opportunities and provide a competitive edge in today's rapidly evolving job market. Moreover, education equips individuals with essential skills, fosters networking opportunities, and facilitates career progression.

However, success isn't solely determined by academic achievements. There exist avenues where formal education isn't mandatory for success. Entrepreneurship, creative fields like art and music, and certain skill-based professions offer pathways to success that don't require traditional education.

Entrepreneurs thrive on innovation and problem-solving, traits nurtured outside the confines of formal education. Similarly, artists and craftsmen leverage their innate talents and creativity to carve out successful careers. Additionally, professions like plumbing and electrical work prioritize practical skills over academic credentials.

It's crucial to recognize that success is subjective and multifaceted. While formal education may pave the way for success in certain fields, it isn't the sole determinant of one's achievements. Individual circumstances, aspirations, and opportunities all play pivotal roles in shaping one's path to success.

Moreover, while examples of successful individuals without formal education exist, they represent a small minority. For the majority, formal education serves as a vital foundation for future endeavors. It provides structure, skills, and knowledge necessary to navigate diverse career landscapes.

In conclusion, the debate over the necessity of education for success is nuanced and multifaceted. While education offers numerous advantages and opportunities, success isn't exclusively reserved for the academically inclined. It's essential to consider individual circumstances and aspirations when navigating educational and career choices.

As mentors, parents, and individuals, let's approach this debate with an open mind and recognize the value of both formal education and alternative pathways to success. By embracing diverse perspectives, we empower individuals to make informed decisions and pursue their unique paths to success.

"The beautiful thing about learning is that no one can take it away from you."

Degrees equal to
Dream Job?

I'd like to share an intriguing counseling experience I had at a school in the southern region. The parent I interacted with was highly academically qualified, boasting multiple postgraduate degrees, including double MA and two PhDs. Despite his impressive credentials, he found himself working as a clerk in the railways, a fact he couldn't quite explain during our session.

During our conversation, the parent expressed a desire for his daughter, who was in the ninth grade, to attain even more qualifications than he had. He believed this would enhance her prospects in the future. However, I couldn't help but wonder why someone with such extensive qualifications was content with a job he didn't enjoy. The parent's satisfaction with his own job and challenges the notion that degrees equate to a dream job.

When I raised this point with him, he admitted to not being happy with his current job but felt obligated to support his family. He harbored aspirations for his daughter to achieve more academically as a matter of prestige.

I gently challenged his perspective, emphasizing the importance of empowering children to pursue their own passions and goals rather than imposing our unfulfilled desires onto them. While parents can offer guidance based on their experiences, forcing children into predetermined paths can lead to resentment and unhappiness.

In essence, while degrees can certainly enhance career prospects, they should be seen as tools to support one's journey toward a fulfilling and meaningful career rather than the sole determinant of success or happiness in the workplace. It's essential for individuals to explore their interests, gain practical experiences, and pursue opportunities that resonate with their passions and values, ultimately leading them closer to their own definition of a dream job.

Ultimately, I urged the parent to consider his daughter's individual aspirations and interests and to support her in making informed decisions about her future. Prestige, I noted, is subjective and should not override a child's happiness and fulfillment.

This experience underscored the need for parents to empower rather than impose their aspirations on their children. By fostering open communication and supporting their children's autonomy, parents can help them navigate their career paths with confidence and authenticity.

"It's not about the degree you get, but the degree to which you care about what you get."

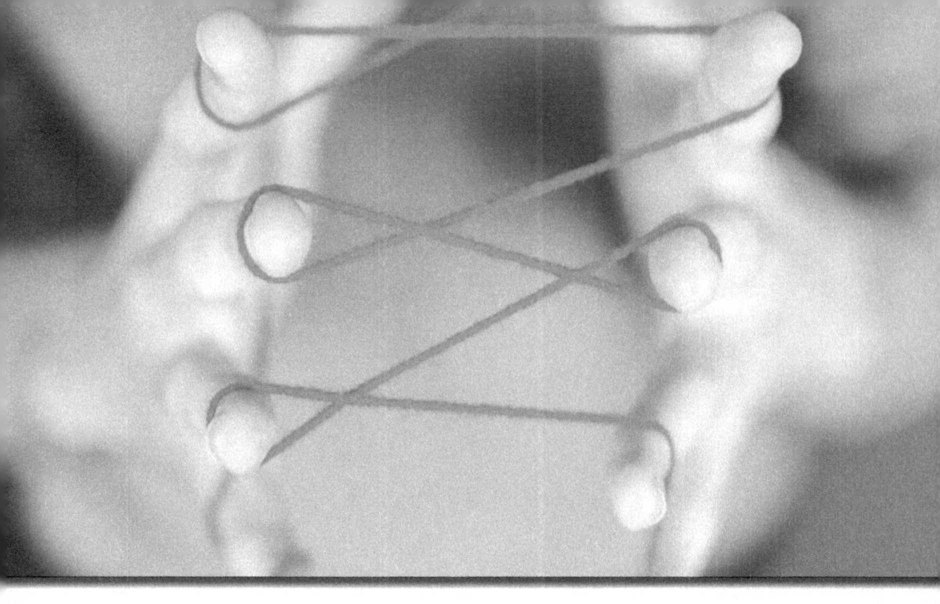

Section 3

Eccentric Expectations

10

Following the Footsteps

I'd like to share a contrasting experience to the one I discussed earlier about the notion that having numerous degrees doesn't necessarily lead to a dream job. In this instance, the dynamic was quite different.

A few years back, I found myself in a counseling session with a parent and their child. While I wasn't familiar with the parent's background, I knew they had completed postgraduate studies. The parent seemed more passive during our conversation, while the child actively engaged with me.

We delved into the child's aspirations and career priorities. To my surprise, the tenth-grade girl expressed a desire to follow in her father's footsteps by joining Christian missionary work. She explained that her parents were pastors, and she wanted to pursue a formal academic path in missionary work.

I needed to understand the academic requirements for such a path and verify that it aligned with the parent's wishes. However, the parent affirmed that the decision was entirely the child's, inspired by the service aspect of their parents' work rather than spiritual preaching.

Upon confirming the child's genuine interest, I offered assistance in acquiring the necessary professional qualifications. While I needed time to gather specific details about academic qualifications, I assured them of my support in navigating this path.

The essence of the experience lies in the voluntary nature of the child's decision and the alignment between parent and child. It underscores the importance of empowering and guiding children based on their genuine interests rather than imposing parental expectations.

Ultimately, the goal is to ensure that children make informed decisions and pursue paths that resonate with their aspirations, avoiding the pitfalls of forced choices and false expectations.

> *"Following in the footsteps of greatness*
> *requires courage, determination, and*
> *unwavering commitment."*

11

Religious Profession vs Professional Career

In a recent interaction with senior intermediate students at a junior college in Hyderabad, a significant dilemma surfaced: the choice between pursuing a religious profession as a career or opting for a professional career in business management and commerce. The focal point of discussion was a highly aspirational student aiming for a career in banking and finance,

juxtaposed with his parents' expectation for him to become a "maulvi," a religious scholar in Islam.

The student, academically inclined and driven, expressed his desire to enter the business and finance sector. However, his parents held steadfast expectations for him to follow the path of religious scholarship, envisioning him teaching in madrasas after becoming a maulvi. The prospect intrigued me, prompting me to delve deeper into the requirements and potential of this religious profession.

Through our conversation, the student revealed that becoming a maulvi entailed a commitment of three to five years, potentially extending to eight, to acquire the necessary knowledge and credentials. Upon completion, one could expect to earn a modest income, teaching in madrasas.

Armed with this newfound insight, I urged the student to consider both sides of the coin: the religious profession versus the professional career. I advised him to have a candid discussion with his parents, presenting the pros and cons of each path. Additionally, I encouraged him to explore the possibility of pursuing his aspirations after completing undergraduate studies, thereby allowing time for both personal growth and parental understanding.

The essence of my advice lay in finding a middle ground, where the student's aspirations and his parents' expectations could harmonize. By initiating a dialogue and presenting a reasoned approach, he could navigate the complexities of familial expectations and personal ambitions.

This scenario underscored a common theme: the clash between parental expectations and individual aspirations. Whether it be religious professions or professional careers, the key lies in understanding, communication, and compromise within the family dynamic.

Reflecting on similar situations, such as a previous encounter with a student aspiring to enter the Christian ministry, I emphasized the importance of empathy, understanding, and mutual respect in resolving conflicts of expectations.

In essence, the decision between religious professions and professional careers transcends mere career choices; it embodies the delicate balance between familial tradition and individual dreams. It is a journey of self-discovery, negotiation, and reconciliation, where aspirations and expectations converge to shape one's path forward.

"To be successful, the first thing to do is fall in love with your work."

Beyond Imagination

I have another experience to share. This student of nineth grade hails from a well-known town in Tamil Nadu, down south. During a group conversation, he approached me and requested a private one-on-one chat. He said, "Sir, could you spare five minutes for a personal conversation?" I agreed, and he suggested we move away to a quieter spot.

This young boy leaned into whisper in my ear, asking if smuggling

could be a viable career. His unexpected question caught me off guard, and I took a moment to gather my thoughts. I replied, "Well, any career revolves around making money. While it is true that smuggling might offer financial gains, it's important to consider its legality."

The boy persisted, referencing a well-known figure—Pablo Escobar or someone similar—who had made a name in the underworld. Despite my lack of familiarity with this person, I felt compelled to address the issue. I told him, "My dear boy, smuggling is not a legitimate career choice. Instead, I encourage you to pursue legal avenues for your future."

It's crucial to guide young minds away from harmful paths, even if they find allure in the forbidden. Smuggling, though tempting in terms of financial gain, carries significant risks and consequences. Let's focus on lawful options that lead to a brighter and more secure future.

The boy persisted, expressing his curiosity about smuggling despite my warnings. He acknowledged that while it might be possible to engage in such activities, legality remained a significant concern. I cautioned him against being influenced by movies, web series, or YouTube content that glamorized illicit paths. Grateful for my advice, he bid me farewell.

Still reeling from the encounter, I sought out the school counselor. I recounted the incident, and she began connecting the dots. It turned out that the boy hailed from a politically connected family in the local area. His father, a prominent figure in the municipal council, had faced rumors and even police cases related to illegal businesses or smuggling. The school counselor speculated that this background might explain the boy's unusual question.

The boy's background shed light on his unusual query. He hailed from a politically connected family, where rumors swirled about his parents' involvement in illicit activities. Perhaps this environment had sparked his interest in unconventional career choices.

I emphasized the importance of legality and encouraged him to explore lawful avenues. It's essential to steer young minds away from harmful paths, even when they find allure in forbidden territories. I hope that boy eventually made the right choices and carved a brighter future for himself.

This experience serves as a reminder that as educators and mentors, we encounter unexpected questions that challenge our perspectives and require thoughtful responses, at times beyond imagination.

"The quality of your life is built on the quality of your decisions."

13

Aspirations vs Dilemma

Titled "Child's Aspiration versus Parents' Dilemma," my recent mentoring session encapsulated a profound exploration of the delicate balance between a child's visionary dreams and the pragmatic concerns of parents. As a career mentor, I found myself drawn into the intricate dynamics of guiding a ninth-grade student

towards defining their career path, while also navigating the parental apprehensions that often accompany unconventional aspirations.

The session commenced with the parent offering insights into their child's unique perspective on art—an introspective inquiry that challenged conventional norms. Witnessing the child's thought-provoking approach to expression, I couldn't help but marvel at the depth of their introspection, which set the stage for a broader discussion on career aspirations.

As the conversation unfolded, the student unveiled a remarkable interest in the futuristic realm of life sciences, particularly in areas such as mind uploading and digital immortality. Despite my initial unfamiliarity with these concepts, I was deeply impressed by the child's bold vision and unwavering determination to explore uncharted territories within the field.

However, amidst the child's visionary aspirations, I sensed a palpable undercurrent of uncertainty and apprehension from the parent—a sentiment that resonated with my own experiences as a mentor and parent. Balancing the child's innovative spirit with the pragmatic realities of career planning became the central focus of our dialogue, as we sought to chart a course that honored both aspiration and practicality.

Guided by the principle of fostering ambition while safeguarding against unfounded fantasies, I emphasized the importance of cultivating a "fail-proof mechanism"—a safety net of alternative pathways within the broader domain of life sciences. By encouraging the child to explore unconventional avenues while maintaining a practical foundation, I hoped to instill a sense of resilience and adaptability that would serve them well on their journey.

Through introspection and empathetic guidance, our session epitomized the transformative power of aspiration, tempered by the wisdom of experience. It underscored the universal struggle of reconciling dreams with reality, of embracing the unknown while seeking stability in familiar terrain—a journey that resonated deeply with both the child and the parent.

In essence, "Child's Aspiration versus Parents' Dilemma" embodied the profound intersection of hope and pragmatism, of vision and practicality. It celebrated the courage to dream boldly while navigating the complexities of career planning—a journey that epitomizes the essence of mentorship and the transformative power of shared exploration.

"The only limit to our realization of tomorrow
will be our doubts of today."

Section 4

Parenting Patterns

14

Fast Track

The recent career workshop I conducted for parents was a pivotal event aimed at raising awareness about the critical aspects of career guidance and planning. It was a  packed session with around 500 parents and their children in attendance, highlighting the importance and urgency of addressing this crucial aspect of education and development.

The workshop delved into the traditional paradigms of career planning, which often revolve around academic excellence in specific subjects such as mathematics or biology. In the conventional approach, students are directed towards streams like PCM (Physics, Chemistry, Mathematics) for engineering or PCB (Physics, Chemistry, Biology) for medicine. However, the session emphasized the need to broaden perspectives and consider a child's holistic development, including their personality traits, aptitudes, and interests, in addition to academic performance.

Parents were encouraged to look beyond the narrow confines of academic scores and explore psychometric assessments as valuable tools for understanding their child's inherent strengths and inclinations. These assessments provide insights into a child's personality, learning style, and potential career pathways, facilitating more informed decision-making regarding their future pursuits.

During the interactive segment of the workshop, a parent raised a pertinent question regarding the perceived lengthy process of career planning. They questioned whether there could be a more expedited approach to help children navigate their career choices more swiftly. In response, I drew an analogy between career planning and childbirth, emphasizing that both journeys require time, patience, and careful nurturing.

Just as childbirth is a journey that unfolds over the course of approximately nine months, career planning is a gradual and evolving process that extends over several years. In the context of childbirth, each stage—from conception to delivery—involves careful monitoring, preparation, and anticipation. Similarly, career planning encompasses various stages of exploration, discovery, and decision-making, each requiring thoughtful consideration and guidance.

During pregnancy, expectant parents invest time and effort in preparing for the arrival of their child. They attend prenatal appointments, gather information about childbirth and parenting, and create a supportive environment conducive to the baby's development. Likewise, in the realm of career planning, parents and children engage in proactive exploration, seeking out resources, information, and guidance to navigate the complexities of the career landscape.

As the pregnancy progresses, expectant parents experience a range of emotions—from excitement and anticipation to uncertainty and anxiety—while eagerly awaiting the arrival of their baby. Similarly, the journey of career planning is marked by a spectrum of emotions, including enthusiasm for new opportunities, uncertainty about the future, and the desire to make informed choices that align with one's passions and aspirations.

Just as the process of childbirth culminates in the delivery of a newborn baby, career planning leads to the realization of professional goals and aspirations. However, both journeys require patience, resilience, and adaptability, as unexpected challenges and uncertainties may arise along the way.

Moreover, just as each child is unique and deserving of individualized care and attention, each individual's career path is distinct and shaped by their interests, talents, and values. Therefore, rushing through the process of career planning, akin to attempting to expedite childbirth, may overlook the importance of thoughtful consideration and reflection, potentially leading to decisions that are not fully aligned with a child's inherent strengths and aspirations.

While technological advancements have accelerated many facets of modern life, career decisions remain deeply personal and multifaceted. Rushing through the process of career exploration and decision-making could lead to uninformed choices that may not align with a child's long-term aspirations and potential.

I underscored the importance of involving children in career exploration from an early age, encouraging them to research various career options, understand industry trends, and reflect on their own interests and values. By starting this process early and allowing ample time for exploration and reflection, children can make more informed decisions about their academic and professional pathways.

Ultimately, the workshop emphasized the need for a balanced and thoughtful approach to career planning—one that considers both academic achievements and personal aspirations. By prioritizing comprehensive research, self-reflection, and informed decision-making, parents and children can chart a course toward fulfilling and meaningful careers that resonate with their unique talents and interests.

"Patience is bitter, but its fruit is sweet."

15

Face Reading

In this episode, I'd like to share an intriguing experience involving a 10th-grade girl and her parents. They came to me seeking guidance on her career path, particularly regarding her academic performance and choice of stream after the 10th grade. The conversation focused on addressing these key questions.

I initiated the discussion by explaining the importance of assessing personality traits and interests to guide career decisions. The conversation lasted about 20-25 minutes,

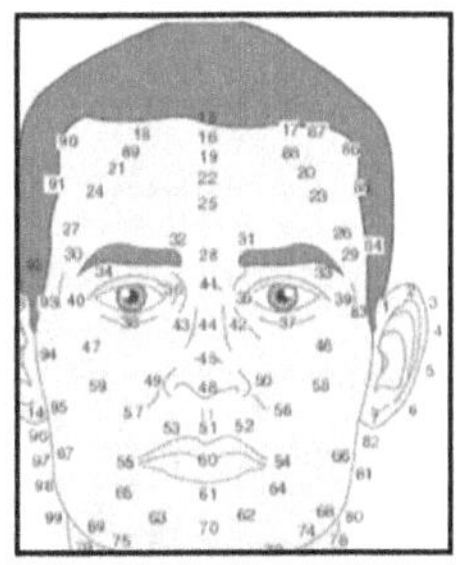

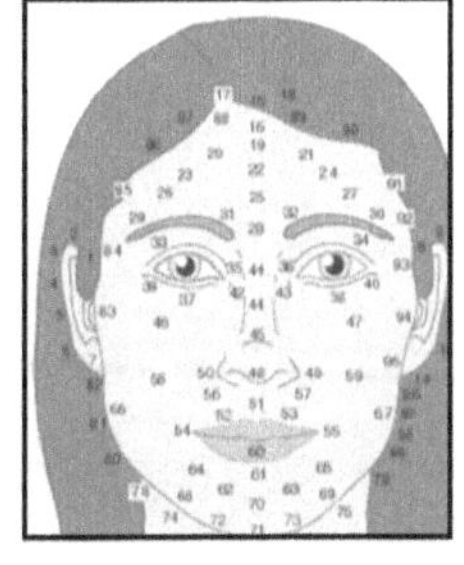

during which the father observed keenly. Eventually, he asked why I couldn't determine his daughter's ideal career by simply observing her facial expressions and body language.

Initially puzzled, I realized he was hinting at face reading, which I found concerning. I clarified that while facial expressions might reveal a person's involvement or genuineness in conversation, they couldn't determine an entire career path. I emphasized the need to consider various factors such as personality, abilities, interests, family expectations, and financial viability.

After further explanation, the father began to understand the importance of a structured, unbiased approach to career guidance. He acknowledged that while facial cues might offer clues, they couldn't replace a systematic assessment process.

This experience highlights the misconception that career decisions can be made solely based on face reading or intuition. It underscores the necessity of a structured, unbiased approach to career planning, considering multiple factors to ensure informed decisions.

As mentors and counselors, it's crucial to guide individuals through a comprehensive assessment process rather than relying on superficial observations. This ensures that career decisions are based on thorough evaluation and consideration of all relevant factors.

"A meaningful career path is discovered through introspection and thoughtful consideration, not superficial observations."

16

Destiny! or Fate!

In this episode, titled "Destiny or Fate," I encountered a thought-provoking scenario during a conversation with a ninth-grade student and her parents about career planning. The objective was to guide the student toward a suitable career based on her aspirations, interests,  and her family's expectations. The student expressed a strong interest in journalism, mass media, and communication, which resonated with her academic inclinations in social sciences.

However, the mother posed a poignant question about destiny and fate, prompted by her own experiences with her elder daughter's career aspirations. She shared how she had encouraged her older child to pursue a career in the public sector, particularly  aiming for the UPSC civil services exams. Yet, despite her efforts and the daughter's dedication, success eluded her in the competitive exams.

This revelation led the mother to question the role of destiny in career choices and outcomes. As I grappled with her inquiry, I emphasized the importance of making informed career decisions based on an individual's personality, abilities, and interests. I underscored the significance of mapping one's nature to potential career paths to minimize the risk of future regrets or feelings of being "not meant for" a chosen path.

By aligning one's intrinsic qualities with career choices early on, individuals can navigate their professional journeys with clarity and purpose. It's crucial to recognize that while destiny and fate may influence our lives in mysterious ways, proactive career planning empowers individuals to shape their own destinies to a significant extent.

The mother's emotional struggle and introspection highlighted the profound impact of parental influence on children's career decisions. It served as a reminder of the responsibility we bear in guiding and supporting young individuals as they embark on their career journeys.

Ultimately, the conversation underscored the importance of balancing personal aspirations with familial expectations and societal pressures. It emphasized the need for open communication, introspection, and informed decision-making in navigating the complexities of career planning and destiny.

In conclusion, while destiny and fate may linger as abstract concepts, proactive career planning enables individuals to carve out meaningful paths aligned with their true selves. By embracing this approach, we can strive for fulfillment and success on our professional journeys, guided by our aspirations and informed choices.

"Fate whispers to the warrior, 'You cannot withstand the storm.' The warrior whispers back, 'I am the storm.'"

17

Choice Mismatch

One particularly intriguing experience, titled "Choice Mismatch," promises to provide valuable insights for my readers.

Let's delve into the past—back in 2018, at a renowned school in Vishakhapatnam, I  had the privilege of engaging with a substantial group of 11th-grade students and their parents. Our conversation spanned 20 to 30 minutes, focusing on the typical topic of career guidance.

The encounter began with a young 11th-grade student, enrolled in the MEC stream (a combination of math and commerce). Accompanied by his tall father, they entered my office. The father was engrossed in a loud phone call as they walked in. As a welcoming gesture, I stood up, greeted them, and offered seats.

Unexpectedly, the father's first question hit me like a surprise punch: "What is your experience? What are your qualifications?" Clearly, he wanted to verify my credentials. I maintained my composure and replied, "Sir, I bring over 20 years of experience—combining my corporate work and career mentoring background."

The father's scrutinizing gaze intensified. Perhaps my youthful appearance, despite my actual age, contributed to his disbelief. My clean-shaven face, denim attire, and semi-formal look didn't scream "seasoned professional." Nonetheless, I persisted, offering them a seat. The father, still on hold with his phone, proceeded to inquire, "What's your name, sir?" I introduced myself as Ram Krishna. His next statement left no room for ambiguity: "Ram Krishna, you'll discuss only Law or Civil Services as potential careers for my son. Everything else is irrelevant."

As the conversation unfolded, it became evident that the father had a fixed agenda. He entered the career discussion with a predetermined mindset: only two options—Law or Civil Services—were acceptable for his son. Any other paths were off the table. And so, our dialogue began.

Rather than a balanced exchange, the father dominated the conversation. He delved into his son's CLAT exam preparation, discussing Plan B scenarios if the exam didn't pan out. College considerations were also on the table.

Typically, breaking the ice with parents and students takes a few minutes. However, in this case, the parent's monologue extended beyond the norm. Despite my efforts to involve the child, he remained silent. For over five minutes, I listened, waiting for an opportunity to contribute.

Finally, I had to assert myself. Addressing the father, I acknowledged his preferences and assured him we would discuss what he wanted. It was an unusual approach, but the only way to capture his attention and engage in a meaningful conversation.

In preparation for the meeting, I had access to a repository containing the child's personality assessment, psychometric evaluation, academic preferences, and information about their abilities and interests. Armed with this knowledge, I aimed to initiate our conversation from a personality perspective. I emphasized to the parent why considering personality traits alongside abilities and interests is crucial when making career choices. Of course, academic excellence and preferences also play a significant role.

As I delved into specific points from the personality assessment, the parent's attention shifted toward me. He even ended his phone call with someone else, growing curious about our discussion. It dawned on me that this parent was unfamiliar with these assessment methods. Despite his clear preconceptions about career preferences, the child remained silent throughout.

I continued explaining, hoping the parent would grasp the importance of personality traits and abilities. However, instead of focusing on development areas constructively, he turned accusatory. "Your counselor says you need improvement," he told his son. My original intention was to provide insights into the child's personality and abilities, emphasizing growth opportunities. Unfortunately, the conversation took a different turn, and we had already consumed 15 minutes of our allotted 20-minute slot.

After the parents' departure, the boy finally spoke up. Apologetically, he said, "Sir, I'm sorry." Intrigued, I asked why he felt that way. His response left me stunned: "If I open my mouth in front of my father, believe me, that would be my last day!" His words were no joke; he meant it quite literally.

Acknowledging his predicament, I assured him not to worry. Now, with just the two of us, I posed a direct question: "What do you want to do? What career path do you envision?" The boy hesitated but then pulled out a folded A4 paper from his pocket. Handing it to me, he said, "Sir, please read this." Unfolding the paper, I discovered a beautifully handwritten article—one that delved into a current affairs topic, relevant and thoughtfully expressed. I couldn't help but commend his views and eloquence.

The boy's revelation left an impression: "Sir, this is what I'd love to do—I want to write, speak, express, and immerse myself in literature. My passion lies in specializing in English and pursuing a career in literature." It was indeed impressive, especially considering the usual career options like engineering or medicine that most students gravitate toward.

Curious, I asked why he hadn't voiced this earlier in front of his father. His response was chilling: "If I open my mouth in front of my father, believe me, that would be my last day!"

His fear was palpable, and it shed light on the tension between parental expectations and personal aspirations.

Despite the pressure to pursue law or civil services, the boy's heartbeat for literature. He had experience in writing—an article he shared during our conversation. I commended his eloquence and encouraged him to explore further. But when I asked about blogs or contributions to the school magazine, he hesitated. "No, sir," he replied. "If my father finds out, it becomes an issue." A familiar struggle—one's passion clashes with parental expectations.

As the boy continued sharing his predicament, I pondered how I could assist him. His resolve was clear: despite his personal passion for literature, he felt compelled to obey his father's wishes and pursue law. Currently, he was diligently preparing for the CLAT exam, even though it didn't resonate with his heart.

The situation was fixed—a parent imposing their desires on a child, perhaps with good intentions. Every parent dreams of their child's success, yet here, the boy's true calling lay elsewhere. I engaged in a conversation with the child, exploring ways to nurture his literary interests.

He hesitantly expressed his uncertainty: "Sir, I don't know if you can offer any suggestions." Determined, I assured him that I would try. Excusing myself, I stepped out of the room, leaving the boy waiting. My destination: the head of the English department. I shared the entire scenario, emphasizing the parent's pushiness and the child's hidden passion.

The department head was already aware of the situation. When I proposed publishing the boy's article in the school magazine—whether quarterly, half-yearly, or annually—the response was positive. "That's a good idea," the head affirmed. "We'll ensure this child's talent receives the visibility it deserves." A heartwarming resolution indeed!

I returned to the student and relayed the plan: he would meet with the head of the English department, who would offer guidance. Curious, I asked how many people knew about his writing. His response: just four or five close friends. I probed further: was he active on social media? Encouragingly, I suggested creating his own blog and sharing his work there.

The boy hesitated. "Who will read my writings?" he wondered. "Why would anyone follow me?" I assured him: "Don't worry; just start." His initial goal: within a month, make sure all 40 students in his class know about his writing. Gradually, his articles found a place in the school magazine. And yes, starting a blog nowadays is easier than ever—plus, sharing it on Facebook would help spread the word.

As our conversation unfolded, the boy's confidence grew. His eyes sparkled with newfound excitement. Once again, he apologized for not speaking up in front of his father. I reassured him: "No need to apologize, my dear." But he sought a promise: that our conversation would remain confidential. I readily agreed. "Between you and me," I assured him. Done!

The boy radiated happiness, and even the parent seemed content—despite the limited choice the boy had in following his father's wishes. I ensured that the student's passion remained alive, providing encouragement along the way. Our initial conversation concluded, but the tale continued.

Six months later, during my return visit to the same school, I encountered the boy again. His eyes sparkled as he rushed toward me, a broad smile on his face. "Thank you," he said, hoping I remembered him. His enthusiasm touched my heart. He led me to the school noticeboard, where one of his recent articles was proudly displayed. Now, everyone in the school knew about his writing.

Although he hadn't started a blog, he shared that he'd been posting his work on Facebook, receiving positive feedback. His CLAT coaching was progressing well, aligning with his father's wishes for a legal career. Despite the compromise, the boy's passion for literature still burned brightly.

Regardless of the specific career path this boy ultimately chooses—whether he becomes a lawyer, a civil servant, or a literature expert—the crucial point is that he found happiness. His spirit remained uncrushed, and he wasn't isolated. His ideas weren't stifled; instead, he was given an opportunity to express himself through writing. This encouragement fueled his faith and hope for the future. As an obedient child, he acknowledged that he would follow his father's wishes, recognizing that he had limited options.

However, this situation calls for deeper conversations with parents. It's not about right or wrong; rather, it's about making informed career choices while considering all relevant factors and stakeholders.

You might wonder: How should parents react? What choices should students make? What role should counselors and mentors play? Each perspective is valid.

Reflecting on this experience, I emphasize that a mismatched career choice can lead to a miserable journey and friction in one's work life.

Parents should listen to their children's interests and aspirations, and children should feel empowered to express themselves. Balancing parental expectations with personal happiness is essential for a fulfilling future.

> *"We grow up in a belief system according to which children should always make their parents proud and happy (instead of making themselves proud and happy) - and that's unfortunately the belief system in most cultures."*

18

Conflicting Interests

Ihave a compelling experience to share, a recent conversation with a student mentee. This young girl just completed 10th grade and her father sought my  guidance for her career. As usual, we conducted assessments before delving into discussions. The consensus leaned toward biology-based careers, preferably non-medical paths, given the child's interests and personality.

However, I discovered something alarming. The mother, adopting an autocratic parenting style, had already enrolled the child in NEET coaching right after 10th grade, without even considering her preferences. The mother's singular vision was for her daughter to become a doctor, fulfilling her own unmet aspirations. On the contrary, the father was open to exploring various career paths for his daughter.

During our discussions, we explored diverse biology-based career options, from immunology to pharmacy. But every time I presented an alternative to medicine, the child's immediate concern was, "Does this career require NEET coaching?" It was evident that she felt cornered by her mother's expectations.

Interestingly, the mother's reasoning for continuing NEET coaching, even if the child opted out of medicine, was to equip her for any entrance examination in the future. However, this approach only added to the child's stress and limited her options.

I gently reminded the mother that NEET coaching isn't a prerequisite for all biology-based careers. It was crucial to empower the child to explore her interests freely, without feeling coerced into a single career path.

Ultimately, the goal is to empower our children to make informed decisions about their futures, without the burden of conflicting expectations. Authoritative and autocratic parenting can lead to negative consequences, undermining the child's confidence and happiness.

Conflicting interests between parents and children often arise when their expectations and aspirations for the child's future diverge. Parents may have specific career paths or life goals in mind for their children based on their own experiences, beliefs, or unfulfilled dreams. On the other hand, children may have their own interests, passions, and aspirations that differ from what their parents envision for them.

These conflicting interests can create tension, stress, and misunderstandings within the family dynamic. Parents may feel frustrated or disappointed if their children do not pursue the paths they have in mind, while children may feel pressured or constrained by their parents' expectations.

It's essential for parents and children to engage in open and honest communication to understand each other's perspectives, values, and goals. Finding common ground and respecting each other's aspirations is crucial for maintaining healthy relationships and supporting the child's personal and professional growth.

Ultimately, the key to resolving conflicting interests lies in fostering mutual respect, empathy, and understanding between parents and children, allowing them to navigate their differences while working towards shared goals and aspirations.

In conclusion, let's strive for a balance between discipline and trust in guiding our children's career choices. Empowering them to make their own decisions ensures their long-term success and fulfillment.

"It is better to bend than to break."

19

Unwarranted Choice

In this poignant episode titled "Unwarranted Choice," I encountered a senior intermediate student, a 12th-grade girl with remarkable aspirations amid challenging circumstances. This young

soul, navigating the complexities of life, was pursuing a Commerce stream and harbored dreams of a career in design.

What set her narrative apart was the immense dedication she poured into her education, overcoming a daily journey that demanded four hours, involving multiple public transport changes in Hyderabad. Her family's socio-economic standing added an additional layer of complexity, as both her parents were nearly bedridden, unable to actively participate in the workforce. Undeterred, this resilient young girl harnessed her natural talent  for knitting and weaving, crafting small handmade items that she sold online, primarily through Instagram. Astonishingly, the proceeds from her creations became a lifeline, supporting her family and contributing to their meager income.

Yet, the family grappled with an orthodox mindset and religious beliefs that posed challenges to the girl's education. The parents, constrained by societal norms, were initially against educating their daughters. However, the elder sister's success in completing some level of undergraduation and securing a job compelled the parents to recalibrate their stance, albeit reluctantly. Despite this, they remained firm in their convictions, pressuring the younger daughter to abandon her education.

As the situation escalated, the parents issued an ultimatum: continue education and leave home or sacrifice education to stay within the family. Faced with an unwarranted choice, this young girl found herself at a crossroads, torn between her aspirations and familial expectations.

During our conversation, the focus shifted from career aspirations to general counseling, as I empathized with the delicate situation she found herself in. I emphasized the importance of finding balance and not allowing emotions to override reason. At just 16 years old, she wasn't yet equipped to navigate an independent life.

I advised her to consider alternatives that would allow her to pursue education without straining family ties excessively. Options such as meeting minimum attendance requirements for exams, exploring open schooling, or opting for distance education emerged as potential compromises. The goal was to foster a dialogue that respected both her aspirations and her family's beliefs.

The underlying issue, beyond this individual story, pointed to societal challenges arising from orthodox mindsets and rigid beliefs. It underscored the responsibility we share, as individuals and mentors, to enlighten such parents about the broader horizons education can offer. While not advocating sweeping social reforms, the episode highlighted the need to address these issues within our capacities.

In essence, the "Unwarranted Choice" exemplifies the delicate balance between personal aspirations and familial expectations, shedding light on the complexity of decisions faced by young individuals in less fortunate circumstances. It serves as a reminder that our collective responsibility includes gently awakening those who may inadvertently hinder the dreams of the younger generation.

"In the end, we only regret the chances we didn't take."

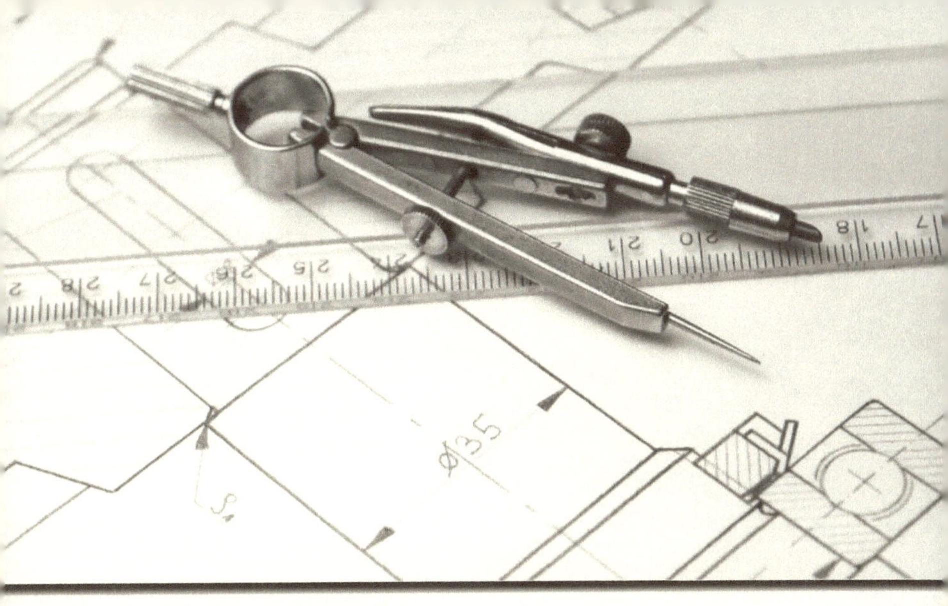

Section 5

Prudent Planning

20

Wise Choice

Allow me to share an intriguing experience involving a parent who made a thoughtful choice to guide her daughter's career path.

The setting is one of Hyderabad's prominent schools, and the child in question is in the ninth grade. I had the privilege of conducting a career workshop, focusing on upcoming careers—specifically unconventional options. The agenda was clear: raise awareness among students about the diverse prospects available beyond traditional choices.

The workshop catered to students from the eighth, ninth, and tenth grades, along with their parents. As the session unfolded, questions arose, and that's when an unexpected participant stepped forward. A parent, who had initially missed the workshop, arrived just in time for the Q&A segment. She introduced herself as a medical doctor—a practicing gynecologist. Her husband, also a doctor, specialized in pediatrics. Together, they ran a local nursing home, boasting a solid reputation. Despite her busy schedule, she apologized for her tardiness, emphasizing that her life had revolved around medicine.

What struck me was her admission: in the past twelve months, she had visited her child's school only once—for a mandatory formality. Yet, on this occasion, she made a deliberate effort to attend the career-related conversation. Her presence warmed my heart; it was a testament to her commitment as a parent.

Returning to the topic, the parent—both she and her husband being doctors—expressed a unique perspective. She approached me during the Q&A session of a career workshop at a prominent Hyderabad school. Her request was straightforward: "Can you suggest any careers other than medicine for my daughter?" This stood out because most doctor parents typically prioritize medical careers for their children.

The parent shared her reasons: over the past year, she had visited her child's school only once—for a brief 10–15-minute formality. Their lives revolved around their four-floor nursing home, where they treated patients' day and night. Personal and family time had become scarce. Determined not to impose their lifestyle on their children, she decided that medicine would not be an obligatory choice for them.

The parent's perspective struck a chord with me. She candidly expressed her reluctance to recommend medicine as a career for her children. Her reasoning was clear: she didn't want them to lead the same all-consuming lifestyle she and her husband experienced as doctors. Their nursing home practice demanded nearly every waking hour, leaving little room for personal or family life.

During our conversation, we explored various science streams beyond medicine and engineering. Not limiting ourselves to just math or biology, we discussed other options in commerce and humanities. The parent left the discussion feeling well-informed about the diverse educational paths available. Her wisdom lay in recognizing that her children shouldn't be compelled to follow the same professional trajectory. Despite their established nursing home, she wanted them to explore their own passions and aspirations.

Indeed, the parents' decision was wise. By allowing their child to explore various possibilities while also discussing the pros and cons of a medical career, they empowered their child.

This experience underscores the importance of enabling children to explore diverse paths rather than merely fulfilling parental wishes. As parents and elders, we should prioritize informed career choices for our children.

*"Balance is a feeling derived from being
whole and complete; it's a sense of harmony.
It is essential to maintaining quality in life
and work."*

21

Peer Pressure

I'd like to share a recent mentoring experience with a 10th-grade student. This student, at just 15 years old, is an accomplished basketball player,

having competed at regional and national levels. In fact, he's on the cusp of representing the highest levels in basketball competitions.

However, his parents face a dilemma. They're torn between allowing him to pursue basketball as a career or focusing solely on academics. The pressure from peers, family, and societal expectations is pushing them towards prioritizing academics, despite initially supporting their son's athletic ambitions.

From the child's perspective, he's open to either path, but his ultimate goal is to pursue higher education abroad after 12th grade. This creates a complex decision-making process for the parents, who are apprehensive about their child's aspirations but also understand the practical challenges of a career in sports.

In our discussions, we weighed the pros and cons of both options, considering academic pursuits both in India and abroad, as well as the potential of a basketball career. Ultimately, the parents lean towards emphasizing academics over basketball, influenced by societal norms and practical considerations.

The key takeaway here is that every family faces unique challenges and must make decisions based on their circumstances. While societal pressures can influence decisions, it's crucial for parents and children to carefully weigh their options and seek expert advice if needed. The goal is to make a decision that aligns with their values, aspirations, and practical considerations, ensuring long-term happiness and fulfillment.

My perspective is that the decision should be made with careful consideration of the child's interests, talents, and long-term goals. While academic success is important, nurturing the child's passion for basketball can also lead to personal fulfillment and growth. It's crucial for the family to communicate openly, seek guidance from mentors, and make a decision that aligns with the child's aspirations while considering practical realities.

Balancing both academic and athletic pursuits can foster a well-rounded and fulfilling life journey for the child.

I hope this story resonates with those facing similar dilemmas and encourages thoughtful decision-making based on individual circumstances and aspirations.

"Be yourself; everyone else is already taken."

22

Inclination vs Choice

I recently had a conversation with a concerned mother about her daughter, who had just completed 11th grade in an international curriculum, majoring in economics and other related subjects. The mother sought guidance on her daughter's future path

after 12th grade, prompting us to embark on a comprehensive career assessment journey.

We decided to conduct a scientific psychometric assessment to gauge the daughter's personality, abilities, and interests, resulting in five career recommendations: media and communication (with a focus on journalism), general management (with a leaning towards human resources or healthcare administration), law (particularly in AI forensic law), hotel management, and economics (with specialization in financial or business economics).

Interestingly, economics, the daughter's initial inclination, resurfaced as one of the top choices. However, after thorough research and reflection, the daughter decided to prioritize economics, psychology, and media and communication, respectively.

It's worth noting the mother's initial skepticism about the process, questioning its value if their original inclination ended up being their final choice. This prompted a deeper discussion about the importance of structured career guidance.

While some may believe that following one's initial inclination validates their decision-making, it's essential to recognize the limitations of relying solely on intuition. True career guidance involves a systematic approach, encompassing psychometric assessments, research, and informed decision-making.

The goal is not to merely confirm preconceived notions but to explore all possibilities objectively. Through this process, individuals gain clarity about their strengths, interests, and potential career paths, ensuring a well-informed decision.

Ultimately, the daughter's journey illustrates the significance of structured career guidance. While her initial inclination aligned with her final choice, it was the result of a comprehensive process, not mere chance.

In conclusion, the value of career guidance lies in its ability to offer clarity and direction, guiding individuals towards fulfilling and sustainable career paths. It's not about blindly following inclinations but about making informed choices that align with one's abilities, interests, and aspirations.

*"Follow your heart, but take your brain
with you."*

23

Informed Risk

I'm enthusiastic about sharing these experiences to raise awareness and offer valuable insights to readers, parents, and students. Sometimes, learning from others' mistakes can be invaluable, but it's also true that new mistakes can always happen.

Now, let's dive into the topic, but before that, I have a question for you: Are you a risk manager or a risk taker? Well, it depends on your perspective. Some may consider themselves risk takers, while others may see themselves as risk managers. The crucial question, however, is: How well do you navigate risks? Do you make informed decisions, or do you take risks blindly?

Let me share two stories about students facing similar dilemmas. The first student is a 10th-grade girl who shows potential in hands-on, engineering-oriented work. Music is also a strong interest for her. Her parents are torn between supporting her engineering aspirations and considering music as a backup plan. They seek advice on coaching institutes for engineering entrance exams, and I stress the importance of informed decisions.

The second student is academically excellent, aiming for a career in medicine. However, the intense coaching environment for medical entrance exams becomes overwhelming for him. Despite his academic prowess, the pressure takes a toll, leading to verbal and physical abuse in the coaching institute.

Both stories highlight the importance of making informed decisions. Whether choosing coaching institutes or career paths, parents must weigh the pros and cons carefully. Coaching can be beneficial, but parents must ensure it aligns with their child's well-being. Blindly following trends or peer pressure can lead to unforeseen consequences.

In both cases, the students faced challenges, but with informed decisions, they navigated through. As mentors and counselors, our role is to empower families to make informed choices, not to dictate decisions. Parents must consider their child's individuality and well-being above all else.

In conclusion, making informed decisions mitigates risks and prepares families for any challenges ahead. It's crucial to prioritize the child's happiness and well-being when navigating career choices. Let's empower our children to make informed decisions and support them on their journey to success.

"You have to risk going too far to discover just how far you can really go."

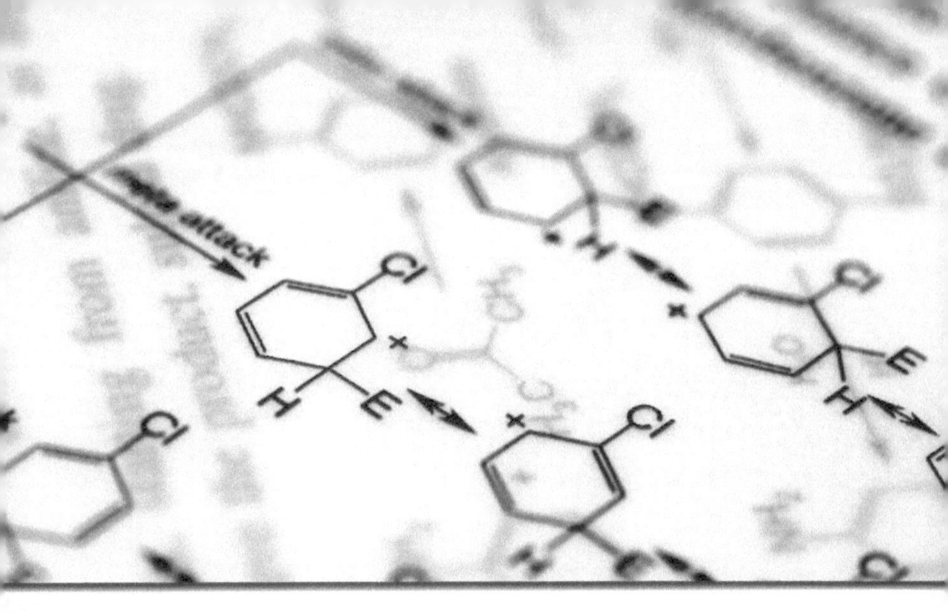

Section 6

Personal Anecdotes

24

Familiarity Breeds Contempt

In a deeply personal reflection, I'm compelled to share an experience drawn from the conversations I've had with my own daughter. My daughter, currently in 11th grade, has been a focal point of discussions revolving around career choices and aspirations. Often, at the culmination of my workshops or individual sessions with

students and parents, I receive heartfelt expressions of gratitude. They commend the guidance provided to their children, echoing sentiments of appreciation. However, there's a poignant realization that strikes a chord - despite echoing similar advice to our children, they seem impervious to our words. This paradox awakens the parent within me, grappling with the intricacies of parenting amidst professional guidance.

I resonate deeply with the sentiment expressed by many parents - the feeling of being unheard when imparting career advice to our children. The adage "a neem tree in your own backyard won't do for medicine; the one that is near is not valued" rings true. Familiarity breeds contempt, rendering our words less impactful. It's a quandary many parents face when attempting to guide their children through career decisions. The dominance of the parental role often eclipses the essence of being a career guide.

The question inevitably arises: should we seek external expertise to assist our children? My unequivocal answer is yes. Despite my professional background in career mentoring and counseling, I've sought external guidance for my own child. Identifying a mentor for my daughter has been instrumental in navigating her career journey. While some may argue that personal experience qualifies us to guide our children, the reality is nuanced.

Having traversed the academic and professional landscapes ourselves, we believe our insights are invaluable. However, the challenge lies in garnering our children's attention and respect amidst familial dynamics. The neem tree in our own backyard serves no purpose to the medicine; familiarity blurs its value.

This analogy resonates deeply with the complexities of parent-child interactions, particularly concerning career choices.

My message is clear: do not hesitate to seek assistance from professional mentors or counselors. This collaborative approach facilitates informed decision-making, fostering confidence in our children's career trajectories. Acknowledging the limitations of parental influence is the first step towards empowering our children to make informed choices.

In conclusion, the journey of guiding our children through career decisions is multifaceted. While our intentions may be pure, seeking external guidance enriches the process and enhances its efficacy. Let us break free from the notion that proximity diminishes value and embrace the transformative potential of professional guidance. Thank you for accompanying me on this introspective journey.

"It takes a village to raise a child."

25

Studies vs Health

In a recent encounter with an old friend, the topic of our daughters' academic pursuits arose, shedding light on the delicate balance between aspirations and health. My friend's daughter, a twelfth-grader, harbored dreams of becoming a doctor, steadfastly committed to

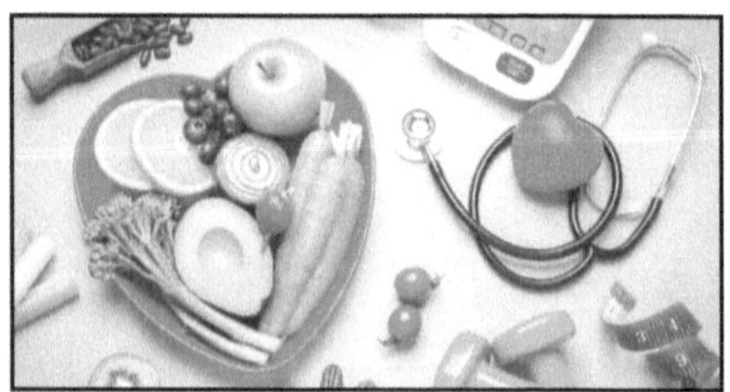

the demanding journey ahead. Meanwhile, my own daughter, a grade below, shared a similar interest in life sciences.

My friend, cognizant of the arduous path to medical school, meticulously guided his daughter by offering firsthand experiences in hospital settings. Despite her unwavering determination, he ensured she understood the physical and emotional toll of the profession. As she excelled academically and in mock medical exams, pride shone in his eyes.

However, beneath the surface of achievement lay a darker reality. Despite her academic prowess, his daughter grappled with vitamin deficiencies, hair loss, and sleep disturbances—a consequence of relentless pursuit. While she thrived academically, her health suffered, prompting concern about the long-term implications of her single-minded focus.

Conversely, my daughter, while navigating her own academic journey, embraced a balanced approach. Recognizing the importance of both aspirations and well-being, she pursued her interests without compromising her health. As my friend's daughter sacrificed her well-being for academic success, it prompted reflection on the true cost of ambition.

The conversation underscored the paramount importance of prioritizing health alongside aspirations. While ambition propels us forward, neglecting our well-being compromises our ability to enjoy success. As parents and mentors, it falls upon us to instill this crucial understanding in our children, guiding them towards a harmonious balance between ambition and health.

The lesson resonates beyond academic pursuits, reminding us that true fulfillment stems from holistic well-being. As we navigate life's complexities, let us not sacrifice health at the altar of ambition, but instead strive for equilibrium in all facets of our journey.

"Balancing your health and studies ensures that you have the energy and focus to excel in both."

Section 7

Out of Bounds

26

Language Barrier

Let me share an intriguing experience involving a fellow counselor from a few years back, during our visit to a school for counseling sessions with students in grades 10 through 12. The

scene was bustling, with back-to-back sessions scheduled, each lasting 30 minutes per student.

One afternoon, a parent arrived with their child, seeking counseling. However, there was a twist. The parent was uncomfortable conversing in English, and Hindi wasn't an option either. They requested to communicate in Telugu, the local language.

Unfortunately, my colleague wasn't proficient in Telugu. Within moments, the discomfort escalated, leading the parent to walk out, citing the language barrier. The situation came to a standstill, prompting the school team to intervene.

Being multilingual, I offered to take over the session in Telugu after completing a few pending sessions. We managed to resolve the issue, and the parent seemed content with the communication in their preferred language.

Later, in a reflective discussion with my colleague, she expressed frustration, advocating for English as the primary language for counseling. However, I emphasized that effective communication transcends language barriers, focusing on ensuring that parents and students understand and value the guidance provided.

While being multilingual isn't always practical, it's crucial to accommodate language preferences to facilitate effective communication. The ultimate goal is to convey guidance in a manner comprehensible to the parent and student.

Language shouldn't hinder the counseling process. Instead, it should prompt us to explore alternative communication methods to ensure clarity and understanding. By acknowledging and addressing language preferences early on, we can streamline the counseling process and better serve our students and their families.

In conclusion, the focus should always be on effective communication and understanding, irrespective of language barriers. I'm committed to sharing more experiences like this to enrich our counseling practice and foster better connections with our clients.

"Language is the blood of the soul into which thoughts run and out of which they grow."

27

Walk the Thin Line

In a ninth-grade scenario, a girl seeks career mentoring, and I, as a mentor, engage in a comprehensive conversation with her. We explore her personality, abilities, and interests to make informed recommendations regarding her future path. 

Interestingly, the girl's family friend happens to be my colleague and indirectly referred her to me for mentoring.

While personal connections are enriching, they can sometimes complicate professional dynamics.

After our initial session, the girl's mother reaches out, expressing concerns about my colleague's involvement in her daughter's academic and career decisions. She feels sidelined as a parent, observing that my colleague's opinions overshadow familial guidance.

Navigating this delicate situation requires a nuanced approach. I acknowledge the family's friendship with my colleague but emphasize the importance of maintaining clear boundaries in the mentoring process. I assure the mother that my focus is solely on the child's best interests and not influenced by personal relationships.

Subsequent conversations with the parents reveal ongoing discomfort with my colleague's level of involvement. They express a desire for greater autonomy in guiding their daughter's journey.

Recognizing the need for professional integrity, I reassure the parents of my commitment to their child's well-being and career development. I encourage open communication and offer support within the scope of my role as a mentor.

Over time, the family takes proactive steps to assert their authority in decision-making, gradually diminishing my colleague's influence. This positive shift underscores the importance of maintaining professionalism and respecting familial dynamics in mentoring relationships.

The key takeaway from this experience is the need to tread carefully and uphold professional boundaries, especially when personal connections are involved. By prioritizing the child's interests and fostering open dialogue, mentors can navigate complex situations with sensitivity and integrity.

> *"In the journey of life, walking the path of integrity often means threading through the labyrinth of relationships with grace and wisdom."*

Be skeptical but learn to listen.

Skepticism

Allow me to share an intriguing encounter I had with a student at a renowned school in Dehradun. As part of a career counseling initiative, I engaged with 10th, 11th, and 12th-grade students, guiding them toward future-ready choices. The sessions were scheduled back-to-back over a couple of days, spanning from 9 AM to 5 PM.

However, there was one student who didn't appear for the morning slot. Curious about the absence, I informed the school team, hoping to reschedule or identify the issue. Their response surprised me: "This student has been free since morning—why didn't he show up?" We resolved to unravel the mystery and ensure he attended the second half of the session. When he finally approached me in the afternoon, he seemed hesitant, dragging his feet.

I initiated the conversation, asking about his name and expressing concern for his absence. The boy hesitantly revealed his reason: he believed I would decide his career for him. He had misunderstood the purpose of our session, assuming that I would make choices on his behalf.

I quickly clarified my role. "I'm not here to decide for you," I assured him. "My purpose is to empower and enable you to make informed decisions." Gradually, he relaxed, realizing that our conversation was about guidance, not imposition. As counselors and educators, we must empower students to shape their own paths, with our support as a guiding tool.

As we conversed, I encountered a fascinating dilemma. His family had high expectations: they wanted him to pursue business management or administration courses and eventually take over the family business. However, this young visionary had different plans—he wanted to carve his own path, prove himself, and explore new horizons.

As we delved into the possibilities, it became clear that he desired both academic knowledge and entrepreneurial creativity. While he considered business-related courses, his true passion lay in creating something unique—an innovative business idea that he could build from scratch. His determination echoed the sentiment that opportunities are boundless, and the sky is the only limit.

A skeptical student who is initially unwilling to have the career conversation with the counsellor, expecting a quick checklist-style conversation, assuming I would decide his career path for him. However, our discussion took an unexpected turn.

We explored his innate potential, considering psychometric assessments, personality traits, aptitude, abilities, and interests. As we delved into the possibilities, he realized that career counseling wasn't about dictating choices—it was about guidance and self-discovery.

The takeaway? Career conversations should empower students, allowing them to shape their own paths. This young visionary left with newfound confidence, ready to prosper on his chosen journey.

Healthy skepticism encourages critical thinking and helps us make informed decisions.

29

Slow & Steady vs Fast & Furious

I have an intriguing experience to share, one that revolves around mentoring a ninth-grade boy for over a year now. Our journey began with psychometric assessments aimed at identifying the best career fit for him. We

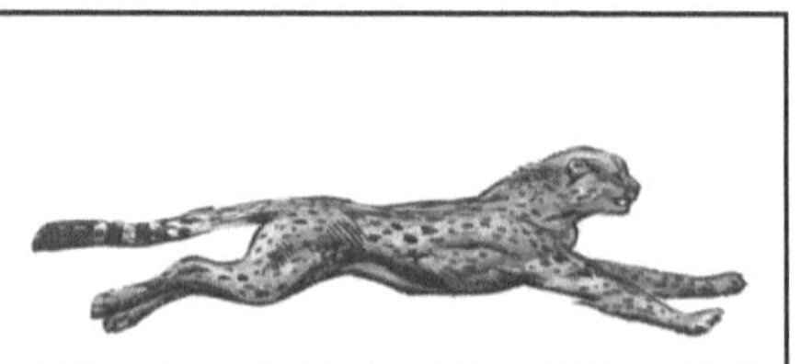

embarked on this path together, his parents deeply involved and supportive.

Recently, amidst a career workshop, I received an urgent message from the boy's parent. Their tone was frantic, hinting at a serious situation involving their child. Despite being in the middle of the workshop, I knew I had to address this immediately. The parent revealed that their child was threatening suicide due to restrictions on gadget usage.

This was a delicate matter, bordering on clinical issues beyond my expertise as a mentor. However, I chose to listen and offer whatever insights I could as a fellow parent and experienced mentor. Understanding the child's personality—a dynamic, challenge-seeking individual—was crucial. Equally important was recognizing the contrasting parenting styles between the father, more lenient, and the mother, stricter and process-oriented.

I suggested diverting the child's attention from gaming by identifying and engaging him in a secondary interest, a strategy that seemed to resonate with the parent. Over time, this approach showed promising results, alleviating some of the parent's concerns and diffusing the immediate crisis.

The key takeaway from this experience is the delicate balance between slow, methodical parenting and the fast-paced, dynamic nature of many children today. Each family navigates this balance differently, and as mentors or counselors, we must adapt our approach accordingly. Building rapport and offering guidance over time is essential in steering children towards their career goals while maintaining harmony within the family dynamic.

In essence, it's about finding equilibrium between opposing parenting styles and recognizing that mentoring is a continual process requiring patience, understanding, and adaptability.

"In the confrontation between the stream and the rock, the stream always wins - not through strength, but through persistence."

Let's Connect

To watch these career conversations on YouTube
Scan the QR Code below:

**To listen to these career conversations on Podcast
Scan the QR code below:**

**About the Author
Scan the QR code below:**

Email – bodduramakrishna@gmail.com
Phone number – +91 98852 44826